A QUESTION AND ANSWER STORYBOOK

Why is the Sky Blue?

and other

outdoor

questions

by Catherine Ripley

illustrated by Scot Ritchie

OWL BOOKS

Why is the Sky Blue? and other outdoor questions

Owl Books are published by Greey de Pencier Books Inc.,
179 John Street, Suite 500, Toronto, Ontario M5T 3G5

Owl and the Owl colophon are trademarks of Owl Communications.
Greey de Pencier Books Inc. is a licensed user of trademarks of Owl Communications.

Text © 1997 Catherine Ripley
Illustrations © 1997 Scot Ritchie

All rights reserved. No part of this book may be reproduced or copied in
any form without written permission from the publisher.

Distributed in the United States by Firefly Books (U.S.) Inc.,
230 Fifth Avenue, Suite 1607, New York, NY 10001.

This book was published with the generous support of the Canada Council,
the Ontario Arts Council, and the Ontario Publishing Centre.

Special thanks to the following people who gave time, thought and advice on the questions and answers
found herein: Jacquie Breedyk and her Grade One class (1993–94); Dr. Randall Brooks, National Museum
of Science and Technology; the Canadian Museum of Nature specialists in collections and research,
namely Dr. Steve Cuumba, Judith Fournier, Michel Gosselin, Cheryl McJannet, Donna Naughton, and
Dr. George Robinson; Christine Demeulemeester; Bill Diehl-Jones, Department of Biology, University of Waterloo;
Dr. Bill James; and finally, Gordon and Marion Penrose. And what would this book be without the editing
talents of Kat Mototsune, Trudee Romanek and Sheba Meland, Mary Opper's wonderful design
and Scot Ritchie's fun illustrations? Nothing. Simply, thank you.

DEDICATION

**For faithful dogs everywhere — especially Rip,
Chimney Sweep, Cinders, Tarfoot, Tucker, Kelsey, Duff, Nikki, and
even though I don't know him personally, Scot's dog...Ollie!**

Cataloguing in Publication Data

Ripley, Catherine, 1957–
Why is the sky blue? and other outdoor questions

(Question and answer storybooks)
ISBN 1-895688-43-4 (bound) ISBN 1-895688-44-2 (pbk.)

1. Natural history – Miscellanea – Juvenile
literature. I. Ritchie, Scot. II. Title.
III. Series: Ripley, Catherine, 1957–
Question and answer storybooks.

QH48.R56 1997   j508   C95-932573-5

Design and Art Direction: Mary Opper

Also available:
Why is Soap so Slippery? and other bathtime questions
Do the Doors Open by Magic? and other supermarket questions
Why do Stars Twinkle? and other nighttime questions

Printed in Hong Kong

A B C D E F

Contents

Why does it smell so fresh after it rains?

Because the air is clean and wet. First the rain washes floating bits, like dust and soot, out of the air. Then the wetness keeps the bits down on the ground, so they don't get in the way of you sniffing other stuff. Wet air carries the smells of the wet trees, grass and earth to your nose better than dry air does. The moisture in the air even makes the inside of your nose wetter, the better to trap all those fresh smells!

Why do worms come out when it's wet?

Because worms like it wet! They always need to stay a little wet or their skin will dry out. When it is sunny, they stay underground in the moist soil. But when it rains, they don't have to worry about the sun drying them up. Out of the ground they squirm to hunt for food. Sometimes it rains after a long dry spell, and all kinds of new plants and animals start to grow underground. They use up a lot of the air that worms need to breathe. Then the worms have to tunnel up and go out above the ground to breathe.

Why do dogs sniff everything?

Sniff-sniff-sniffing is a dog's way of checking things out. A dog's nose can smell things about 40 times better than your nose can. By sniffing, a dog can tell who has been around its home area recently. It can tell if there is another dog nearby. It can tell if the animals it meets (and that includes you) are afraid or happy. A dog also sniffs to find food or to hunt down an interesting-smelling animal, such as a rabbit or — *meow* — a cat!

Ow! How does my cut stop bleeding?

It's a sticky story. As soon as you cut yourself, parts of your blood called platelets start to gather. They stick to each other and to the edges of your cut, forming a thin cover over it. If the cut is big, the platelets may need extra help to stop the bleeding. Along comes fibrin to the rescue. Fibrin is another special part of your blood. It weaves a criss-crossing tangle of long, sticky strands over the cut. Then the strands dry out to make a scab. The scab acts like a bandage, and lets new skin grow underneath. So whatever you do, don't pick at it!

Why do dandelions turn white and fluffy?

So they can make more dandelions! Every dandelion bloom is made up of more than a hundred tiny yellow flowers. A seed forms inside each flower, and gets attached to a long stalk. At the top of the stalks are white tufts. When the yellow petals fall off, all you see is a white ball of fluff. The fluffy tufts are like little kites, each carrying a seed. Along comes the wind, and carries the tufts and their seeds far and wide. The seeds get spread all around, and every seed could grow into a new dandelion.

Why is the sky blue?

Because of scattered blue light waves. Believe it or not, clear light is made up of all the colors in the rainbow — red, orange, yellow, green, blue, indigo and violet. These colors travel in waves. When light hits things, some of the color waves are soaked up, and others bounce off. Whatever waves bounce back to your eyes, those are the colors you see!

High in the sky, the waves of light from the sun hit the air. Air is made up of different gases in tiny, tiny bits called molecules. The blue light waves bounce off these bits of air, and scatter all over the sky. So when you look up, it's blue as far as you can see.

What's that white line in the sky?

It's a trail of ice! It shows you where a jet plane has been. Jet planes have engines to make them move. As the engines work, they let off exhaust that includes water so hot it's like steam coming out of a kettle. When the hot exhaust hits the air outside the plane, the steam cools and turns into water droplets. A second later, the water droplets turn into ice in the fre-e-e-e-zing cold air way up high. These little pieces of ice make a long, white trail behind the plane as it moves.

Why do I feel funny inside when I swing?

Because you're out of balance. It all starts deep in your ears. Messages go from here to your brain. They tell your brain which way you're going and how fast you're going. That's how you keep your balance. When you swing, your body changes its place so fast, the messages can't keep up. Your brain gets a little confused. And when your brain is a little confused, you might feel mixed up inside. The same thing can happen on a roller coaster or even an elevator — whee!

Why do some rocks sparkle?

Because parts of the rock are as smooth as a mirror. Even if a rock looks rough, some of its very small parts can be smooth and flat. When light hits something smooth, some of it bounces off. Just think of how light shines off a mirror. And the more smooth parts the light has to bounce off, the more sparkles it makes. So rocks with lots of little smooth parts really sparkle and shine.

Why do birds sing?

They're talking! If birds sang in words, you'd hear a lot of different messages. In springtime you might hear a male bird's song that says both "Stay away" and "Come and be my sweetie." To other male birds, it's a message to keep out of the singing bird's area, but female birds hear the same call as an invitation to come right in! Birds sing out all kinds of messages. Baby birds call "I'm hun-hun-hungry, Mom and Dad!" Birds in a flock will call to stay together, singing "I'm here, but where are you?" Some birds will even warn each other of danger, calling "Watch out, watch out wherever you are!" All in bird talk, of course.

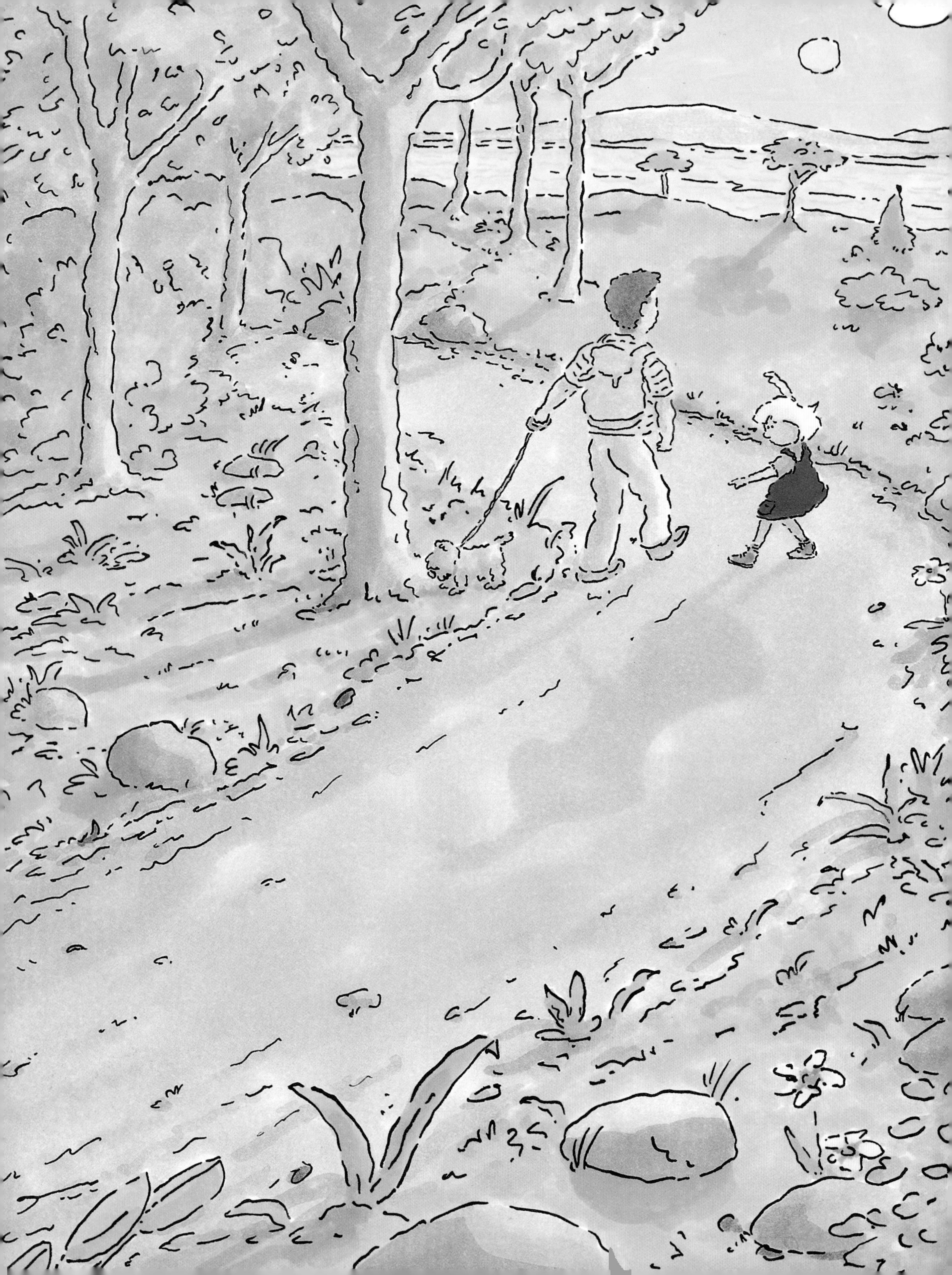

What's a shadow?

It's where light isn't. Light can't travel through things that get in its way. For example, when sunlight hits you, it's stopped by your body, while all around you it reaches the ground. Where you block light from reaching the ground, a dark shape is formed . . . your shadow! It goes with you everywhere — see for yourself on a sunny day.

Where do puddles go?

Up, down, and all around. Sometimes a thirsty animal will lap up some of the puddle water, so the puddle gets smaller. Much of the water seeps down out of sight into the soil. When it stops raining, what's left of a puddle starts to dry up. The water floats away into the air all around, like water from wet clothes hanging up to dry. Going, going, gone!

Outdoor Bits

Some clouds look like giant cotton balls. Just right for jumping into? Not really! Jumping into a cloud would be like jumping into fog — cold, damp, and clammy. Clouds are made of millions and millions of tiny drops of cold water, and sometimes tiny ice crystals, too.

It's raining . . . hamburgers? Raindrops are nice and round way up high in the clouds. But as they fall to Earth, the air pushing against them flattens them into mini-hamburger-shaped drops!

Have you ever noticed that dogs pee a little in a lot of places? Like their relatives, the wolves, dogs do this to mark out an area as their home. When other dogs sniff these spots, they know they have to behave in this dog's home area, get out, or fight to stay and be top dog.